New Towns: Laboratories for Democracy

Report of the Twentieth Century Fund Task Force on
Governance of New Towns

Background Paper by Royce Hanson

The Twentieth Century Fund/New York/1971

Library of Congress Catalog Card No. 71-169197
SBN 87078-124-3
Copyright © 1971 by The Twentieth Century Fund, Inc.
Manufactured in the United States of America

Foreword

Both the plight of the nation's central cities and the blight of its sprawling suburbs have focused increasing attention on the development of new towns. A good deal has been written about various aspects of new towns—their prospects for esthetic and rational planning, their provision of community amenities and facilities, their promise for giving their residents a richer and fuller life. But the governing of new towns has received very little attention, although without adequate machinery to ensure effective democratic processes and procedures there is a danger that these towns will not achieve the more livable environment that is their objective.

The independent Task Force on Governance of New Towns brought together by the Twentieth Century Fund has concentrated its deliberations on this neglected aspect of new-town development. While the Task Force was primarily concerned with formulating machinery for urban areas that are still largely on the drawing boards, many of its recommendations can apply to existing and established urban areas where government, like physical surroundings, is in decay. As the Task Force saw it, new towns can serve as demonstration laboratories for new approaches to more democratic local government. Successful procedures might then be adopted by existing localities.

This approach to the problem of governance emphasizes the view of the Task Force that new towns are not the answer to all the urban problems plaguing the nation. It may be beguiling to consider scrapping the old, but new towns cannot be regarded as a realistic alternative to either cities or suburbs. Rather they offer opportunities for experimentation that may ultimately prove of greater benefit to older, entrenched localities that have been either slow or reluctant to innovate and change. In fact, the Task Force points out that new towns should not be considered as separate and apart from existing cities. On the contrary, it points out that new towns take many forms and may well be considered as part of present cities or metropolitan areas. Whatever the form of local government, the recommendations of the Task Force are directed toward more effective and democratic government.

The Fund, which has a number of studies under way dealing with the "urban crisis," is grateful to the members of the Task Force who gave so much time and thought to a problem that has been largely overlooked. In a real sense, their work was a pioneering one. The Task Force report is accompanied by a factual background paper setting out the issues involved in local governance that was prepared by Royce Hanson, who is presently president of the Washington Center for Metropolitan Studies. Their combined work should be of great value not only to those with a special interest in new towns but to all those who have are interested in the survival and prosperity of America.

M. J. Rossant
June 1971

Contents

Members of the Task Force

Marilyn Gittell
Director
Institute for Community Studies, Queens College, New York

Randy Hamilton
Executive Director
Institute for Local Self Government, Berkeley, Calif.

Alan F. Kiepper
City Manager
Richmond, Va.

John Levering
Director of Institutional Relations
The Rouse Company, Columbia, Md.

Hubert G. Locke
Metropolitan Fund, Inc., Detroit, Mich.

William J. Nicoson
Director
Office of New Communities Development, Department of Housing and
Urban Development, Washington, D.C.

Robert C. Weaver, *Chairman*
Former Secretary of Housing and Urban Development; now Professor of
Economics, City University of New York

Royce Hanson, *Rapporteur*
President
Washington Center for Metropolitan Studies, Washington, D.C.

REPORT OF THE TASK FORCE

The Democratic Promise of New Towns

As governments and concerned citizens in the United States seek solutions to the problems of urban growth, new towns are emerging as promising alternatives to congested central cities and sterile suburbs. While new towns have played an important role for some years in European efforts to cope with overcrowded cities and the need for industrial relocation and redistribution of population, they represent a relatively new form of urban development in the United States. In terms of comprehensive planning they go considerably beyond any of the types of planned towns in America's urban history—its frontier cities, its utopian settlements, its greenbelt and atomic towns.

This Task Force was formed to study the social and political issues inherent in the planning and development of new towns and to make recommendations for new organizational forms that will stimulate full citizen participation in their governance.

WHAT ARE NEW TOWNS?

With the growing popularity of the new-town idea, many real estate promotions will be paraded under its banner even though they meet few, if any, of the criteria for an authentic example. It will therefore be useful at the outset to provide a clear and precise definition of what the Task Force regards new towns to be and to indicate what they might realistically be expected to accomplish in the American context.

A new town is not merely a large development. It is large, but size alone does not make a settlement a new town. It has many inhabitants, but numbers alone do not make up a new town. Consciously designed to meet the needs and problems of urbanism, a new town must contain a diverse population, possess a strong economic base and offer a wide range of employment opportunities in a variety of occupations and industries. In essence, then, a new town must offer all the appurtenances and advantages of existing cities without their glaring disadvantages.

Inherent in the concept of a new town is a recognition that the many parts of the urban system are interdependent and that the new town must contribute to the processes of economic and social integration. Through intelligent, comprehensive planning the new town offers a means of increasing and improving housing and employment opportunities as well as social relationships. It is designed to bring homes closer to jobs and people closer to nature. At the same time, its purpose is to reduce urban distance, isolation and the social and psychological costs of city living. Thus new towns provide "life support systems"—those community amenities, facilities and services that broaden opportunity, add beauty and variety, advance culture and promote well-being.

New towns are by their nature experimental. They offer the nation an opportunity to see what can be done by both public and private sectors to build better cities and foster a better way of life. They encourage innovation in design, building technology, services, social programs and governance.

A review of existing "new-town" developments in the United States convinces the Task Force that very few meet these criteria or are even seriously engaged in the process of achieving them. New developments that are primarily residential suburbs in character, or company towns that fail to achieve a balance between residential and other land uses, do not qualify as new towns. But those few that may fairly be called new towns offer an exciting glimpse of what can be done.

We endorse no single model. On the contrary, we think that a pragmatic, flexible approach to the nation's new towns is necessary. New towns of different sizes and with varied relationships to existing cities and regions need to be developed.

Although some *free-standing* new towns may well be desirable, we regard as a misconception the often expressed notion that a new town must be free standing—self-contained and separate from existing cities or metropolitan areas.

The construction of some new towns as *satellites* of major metropolitan centers should be encouraged as an economical way to organize urban growth in order to prevent wasteful and ugly sprawl.

Similarly, new towns can take shape within the borders of existing metropolises. With their commitment to diversity, economic balance and high-quality services, such *new towns in-town* offer an effective and humane approach to redevelopment strategy for the inner city. They also allow for imaginative use of large vacant tracts within a city. In some cases it may be possible to use a combination of new towns in-town and satellite new towns to assist in meeting the housing and employment problems of a metropolitan area.

It is also possible that *add-on new towns* attached to existing small cities will serve as a means of attracting industry and encouraging diversified economic growth within a region. "Adding on" makes feasible effective use of existing city infrastructure and economic resources.

There are numerous places where new towns of various types and sizes could or should be built in response to national, state or regional development policies. The 1970 Housing and Urban Development Act, passed some months after this Task Force began its deliberations, encourages such a variety of applications of the basic new-town idea.

THE HOUSING AND URBAN DEVELOPMENT ACT OF 1970

Indeed, the passage of the new legislation makes even more urgent the mission of this Task Force. Title VII of the act declares new towns to be key elements in national urban growth policy; it supports this declaration by making assistance available both to state and local public agencies and to private developers in the development of new towns. It creates a Community Development Corporation in the Department of Housing and Urban Development to administer the new-town program.[1] Federal assistance not only includes direct federal loans during the initial development of new towns. It also offers grants to cover the initial costs of providing public services prior to completion of permanent arrangements, supplementary grants for community public works and facilities, and special help to public and private developers of new towns in the use of advanced technology and in social and environmental planning.

The criteria for eligibility under the act are in keeping with the Task Force's definition of new towns. For a proposed new town to be eligible for assistance, it must be feasible in terms of its potential for economic growth. Its plan must include adequate public, commercial and community facilities and services and a substantial amount of low-income and moderate-income housing; it also must give promise of enhancing the natural and urban environment and contributing to the welfare of the surrounding area. The plan must demonstrate that the developer will make use of advanced technology with respect to land use and materials and methods of construction and that he will make provision for most of the activities normally associated with a city. A new town's development program is expected to be consistent with comprehensive area plans and to receive the necessary approval of state and local authorities.

THE NEGLECT OF THE ISSUE OF NEW-TOWN GOVERNANCE

A national commitment to achieve a livable urban environment is incomplete without an equal commitment to make that new environment democratically governable.

Local governments in the United States are often inadequate to deal with the fiscal, service and political problems that confront them. Both cities and suburbs "muddle through" with outmoded, disorganized and underfinanced governments inherited from a simpler age. The need for developing new forms of local government is compelling, and the opportunity the new town offers for developing new ways of engaging citizens constructively and effectively in governing themselves in the urban environment should be obvious.

But though some innovative thinking has been directed toward providing for adequate administrative and financial machinery to plan and build new towns, almost all theorists and developers of new towns have neglected the problem of governance. This neglect extends from the planning phase on through the development of the town and imposes serious limitations on its potential as a functioning urban system after its completion and occupancy.

Recommendations

Because of the neglect of the issue of the democratic government of new towns and because we believe that **new towns provide the nation with a unique opportunity to develop and demonstrate effective methods of governing urban areas,** this Task Force makes the following recommendations:

1. New towns should become laboratories for testing new forms and processes of local self-government.
2. New towns should experiment with different and novel means of broadening and strengthening participation by people in planning, developing and governing their urban environment.
3. From the first stages of settlement, new towns must have a diverse population and a broad range of economic and social activities. Development plans should recognize this objective as a precondition for democratic communities.
4. State and local governments, taking full advantage of Title VII of the Housing and Urban Development Act of 1970, must create the capability to plan and develop new towns either alone or in partnership with private developers. States should adopt imaginative legislation to assure that new towns realize their full potential for self-government.

New towns should become laboratories for testing new forms and processes of local self-government.

While it may not be appropriate or even possible for every new town to have a government of its own until it is well populated, the plan for each new town should provide for development of the governmental, civic and social institutions necessary to enable it to operate as a democratic community.

One of the most important contributions that new towns can make to the general improvement of local government is to devise ways of adjusting governmental institutions to population and other changes. Initial civic planning should not be rigid, but it must provide rudimentary mechanisms and processes which can later be changed or modified to meet the desires and needs of its residents. It is important that the new town not be embalmed with a set of institutions that, however brilliant in theory, will not work in practice. Instead, each mechanism for planning and governing should be carefully thought out, tried and evaluated.

When a new town is started, there may be no residents on the site. Later the population will grow rapidly. Services and the basis for participation by newcomers must accordingly be provided if the town is to function democratically. It may be possible to establish in the planning phase a public agency that can serve as a transitional government.

One fairly simple approach would be to designate the new town a borough or service district and to create a board of public trustees to govern until it could be replaced by an elected council. The parent governmental jurisdictions should gradually delegate their powers to the borough. The trustees and later the new-town council could serve in an advisory capacity to the developer and parent jurisdictions or even provide an increasing number of directors on the board of the development corporation. This measure would provide constructive and effective citizen participation in the development process.

The creation of boroughs with delegated powers would also help to assure the carrying out of the new-town plan without premature incorporation and the consequent vesting of full zoning power in a municipal government. This approach would permit early citizens to participate in the planning and development processes but would prevent their gaining political control of the new town before it is well populated and a permanent governmental structure can be adopted. As citizens of both the new town and its parent jurisdiction, they conceivably could exert enough pressure to stop development. It is more likely, however, that a borough council would be in a strong position to bargain with the parent jurisdiction and the developer to make mutually satisfactory accommodations.

From the developer's point of view, the creation of a governmental body with some revenue powers could facilitate public financing of needed capital improvements and the services that make living in the new town desirable. Even more important, providing an official mechanism for participation would give citizens a sense of shared responsibility in the successful completion of the town. The citizens would become more than mere consumers and would begin to share the costs and problems of creating a better way of life. Their participation might entail some deviations from the original plan and challenge some assumptions and attitudes about preferences, but it would make for a more realistic planning process and a more functional and livable town.

Where it is neither feasible nor possible to create transitional public agencies, homeowners' or community associations may provide an alternative way of furnishing some community services and amenities and serving as a channel of citizen participation in new-town affairs. If such "private governments" are established, it is essential that provision be made for equitable participation in them by renters and other "nonowners" who also have a significant interest in their environment. Furthermore, since such organizations are usually controlled by the developer, at least in the initial stages, careful planning is required to permit a fairly rapid and smooth transition of power to the residents through the formation of a new-town government.

Just as we do not think in terms of a single and simple model for new towns, we do not believe that there is a "one best way" to govern them. We feel, however, that **the ultimate establishment of a general purpose government should be encouraged for all public functions,** since such governments provide a comprehensive political system within which conflicting interests can openly contend for power and resources. A general purpose government is contrary to the practice in many states, where such specialized activities as education are governed and financed by special districts. Some new towns may wish to retain traditional separations. But the Task Force believes that the fewer restrictions placed on the scope of its power, the greater the options available to a new-town government.

The new town offers an opportunity to experiment with the concept of "universal powers" adopted in some European countries, whereby municipalities may do whatever is not denied them rather than only what is expressly permitted, which is usually the case in the United States. This arrangement would make it possible for new towns to "share" the powers of superior units of government so long as the exercise of these powers did not conflict with broader public policy. In some states this sort of governmental arrangement might require incorporation of the new town as a municipality. If so, there is a need for greater flexibility than is now customary in municipal charters and in the laws applying to new towns. Such latitude would permit experimentation that could result in better governmental processes applicable not only to other new towns but to established urban areas.

Procedures for amending the new-town charter should be relatively simple. It may be desirable for the state to review the charter periodically to make sure that it gives the town government sufficient powers to deal with its problems. A state new-towns review commission, which is suggested later in this report, might perform this task.

As an alternative to incorporation as a municipality, a state or an urban county could establish a special type of political subdivision for a new town and give it broad self-governing powers to be exercised through its own elected officials. Such a "near municipality" could perform the functions of an incorporated city in a rural county or share powers and functions with an urban county or a city. This approach would have the advantage of facilitating boundary changes without tedious annexation procedures. It would make a town more flexible than the traditional home-rule municipal corporation in its structure, the scope of its powers and the methods of financing and providing services. If the new town proper is politically interdependent with adjacent developments it might even be useful to combine them in a single new type of political subdivision.

In other cases a new town could exercise both those powers given to it by specific laws and those functions delegated to it by the state or by other local governments. If the parent local jurisdiction were reluctant to share its responsibilities the state could require it to do so. The specific powers of a new-town government might include contracting for services provided to it or contracting to perform services for other governments, community corporations or its own political subdivisions; providing an official means of expressing the opinions of the new town's citizens on intergovernmental matters; and serving as a special taxing area for raising revenues to enable it to furnish additional services. The state or parent government could retain supervisory powers in keeping with its broad interest in new-town affairs.

As a means of furthering democratic participation, the shared power approach offers a more complete urban political experience than most independent municipalities now provide because the government of a new town thus cannot disassociate itself from the affairs of its parent jurisdiction.

A wide variety of other approaches could also be employed in new towns. New towns in-town could undertake experiments in political decentralization; some publicly sponsored new towns could be organized on cooperative or condominium principles, with residents retaining "shares" in common areas or in industrial and commercial land that might yield substantial revenues for reinvestment in public facilities or services.

CITIZEN PARTICIPATION IN PLANNING, DEVELOPING, GOVERNING

New towns should experiment with different and novel means of broadening and strengthening participation by people in planning, developing and governing their urban environment.

Implicit in the conventional wisdom about new towns is

the idea that planning and development come first, democracy later. This need not—and would not—be the case if concern for the growth of democratic institutions and participation of citizens in decision-making were accepted as necessary from the outset and if the planning and development processes were designed to accommodate it.

The neglect of democratic participation in new-town development stems in part from the fears of developers, whether public or private, that a plan subject to all the trials and openness of democratic processes may be impossible to implement, given the time-cost factors and the difficulties of achieving the necessary rationality and balance in land use. The developer may also fear that too much democracy or too much control by local government during the development process will interfere with a well-drawn and already approved plan, especially if the first residents should be opposed to some parts of it. Some new-town developers therefore discourage early municipal incorporation that would give residents power to make planning and zoning decisions and thus could upset the developers' financial position.

There is obviously tension between building a new town and fostering democracy in it. Engaging citizens constructively in planning can delay construction schedules. But with creative and thoughtful approaches to this problem, citizen participation can be made complementary and reinforcing to the development process. New-town planning and development is too important to be left completely to developers and professional planners and too complicated to be left to citizens alone.

Participation by residents or prospective residents provides the developer different perspectives from his own or those of his professional staff. The citizens of a new town have an evident economic and social stake in its development, and the outcome is likely to be better if they have some influence over it and some responsibility for it.

New towns also offer unusual opportunities for community participation through private and public employment and through training and service programs. Both developers and citizen participants should cooperate in devising programs that broaden economic opportunities for area residents who can help build the new town and for those who will inhabit it.

13

The objective of citizen representation and participation in new-town planning is to protect the public interest and to ensure that the interests and concerns of present and future residents are taken into consideration in initial planning and can influence each subsequent stage of development.

Participation in the Planning Phase and During Development

Citizen participation should begin with the planning phase, both to protect the public interest in new-town development and to lay the groundwork for democratic processes. Planning of new towns without some form of participation is unlikely to remain politically feasible as increasing numbers of people recognize that the employment of public resources for new-town development is of direct concern to them. Perhaps the only way to make new towns a major element in an urban growth policy is to provide opportunities for broad participation in the planning stage.

What is done during the planning phase sets in motion forces that will greatly affect what can be done later. The injection of differing interests at this stage is more likely to result in a workable plan, however sketchy or chaotic at first, for development of social and political institutions than if it is left to chance or a single interest.

The nature and the mechanisms for citizen participation in new-town planning can take many forms. In some cases a system of public and official hearings and review of proposed plans might be adequate; as a minimum, private developers should seek the views of citizens' groups in the areas where they plan to locate new towns. In others, a body of citizens, aided by professional planners, might be empaneled to participate in the planning process. In an in-town or add-on new town, it may be more appropriate to establish a new-town district whose residents or governing board could elect official participants to the board of the development group. Alternatively, the board of the new-town district could advise the developer on behalf of its constituency.

In the planning of satellite and free-standing new towns whose development sites are sparsely populated, the planning and development group might be required to include a number of "trustees for future residents" appointed by a governor, mayor or local governing body. These trustees could serve as proxies for the future population and could be replaced on a predetermined schedule as the community became populated. Or the parent jurisdiction might be represented on the board of the development corporation if it did not find indirect participation—through regular governmental processes—adequate.

A new town might conceivably employ several forms of participation that could progress, as the town develops, from simple devices such as hearings or advisory groups to formal government.

The Role of Physical Organization

The developer, the physical designer and citizen participants in new-town planning must all be aware of the political implications of neighborhood composition and services so that the physical organization can be used to strengthen grass-roots democracy. Use of "villages," "clusters" and "neighborhoods" as the design base of a new town suggests one foundation for a formal political system. The ecumenical use of religious facilities would foster different political coalitions and conflicts than separate places of worship in different locations. Village and town centers, community centers and schools can all be sited and designed to facilitate political participation. The availability of public meeting space invites broad political intercourse that might otherwise be stifled.

A system of representation in a new town that builds up from the block or apartment building to the neighborhood, village and town can offer a means of political access, communication and accountability that is very difficult to establish in an unplanned suburb or a nondescript city district. Various systems of representation, including combinations of single-member districts and at-large elections, should be tried.

Frequently the interests of low-income groups and racial minorities are not represented or are underrepresented in local government. This is because electoral constituencies are often too large to reflect minority sentiments sharply. The use of villages as constituencies for the election of new-town council members could open avenues for the recruitment of new leaders from groups too small or too poor to compete effectively on a citywide scale. This method would offer broader access to the system and, of special importance to low-income groups, would create more direct roles in public affairs requiring less time and money to participate. Alternatively, elections at large for a new-town council could be supplemented by the use of village or neighborhood councils as integral parts of the system of participation, communication, representation and delivery of services, thus enhancing the range of political opportunity and experience.

Channels and Resources for Effective Citizenship

The new town must provide the channels for participation through which all elements can have a voice.

A strong voluntary sector. Formal political structures may vary, but the basic strength of democracy is always amplified by numerous voluntary associations involving a large number of citizens. Voluntary associations may be based on neighborhood or community; they may focus on youth services, education, child care, police protection, taxes, commuter transportation or refuse collection; or they may cater to business, occupational, professional or consumer needs. Special-interest groups should be considered important participants in and a complement to the official decision-making apparatus, serving to make the latter responsive and accountable for decisions on public issues. The parent-teacher association, the chamber of commerce, the bar association, labor unions, tenants' councils, cooperatives and the garden club are all important ingredients in the democratic mix. While community groups should not be planned artificially, their organization should be fostered.

Communications. Because new towns undergo rapid change, an exceptional local information system is needed to keep pace. It is axiomatic that information is an essential ingredient for effective participation at the local level. Unfortunately the economics of the mass media restricts coverage of local affairs. But some new towns are beginning to alleviate this problem through use of community antenna television

(CATV) channels to transmit local news and events and to hold televised town meetings. This device can involve many citizens who would not otherwise participate in local affairs. Creative use of CATV and print media, combined with a few well-structured polls or surveys, should also familiarize public officials with the needs and aspirations of the population they serve.

Misinformation and rumor about development plans, public services or the like can be especially troublesome in a new town. Service complaints are common, and knowledge about the local government may be limited or even distorted. The establishment of a citizen's information service or an ombudsman's office at an early stage in a new town should minimize such problems. Such an office could serve as a complaint center and could supply information on government or private services and on community planning and development.

Community education. The citizen needs to know more than where to complain. An informed and active citizenry also requires a continuing education program in order to develop skills in the analysis of community problems. Some knowledge of budgets, building plans, zoning criteria and educational jargon is needed. Politics for most citizens will remain a spectator sport in either an old city or a new town, but both the number and the level of competence of activists can materially affect quality of a new town's development. It should be possible to use local educational institutions to maintain a relatively low-cost civic action and research program that would systematically sample attitudes and concerns, define public problems and develop programs for resolving them. Such a program might help students to learn about their community as well as help citizens and organizations to find solutions to particular problems.

A civic action and research program could be most useful in relating local political institutions to the pace of development. By gauging the need for change in light of altered circumstances, it could advocate incremental adjustments that would prevent crises or breakdowns. The pressure of ongoing business will be too great for the new town's council, the parent government or the developer to fully consider the implications of civic feedback and emerging needs for change;

even in a new town with effective citizen participation, relationships will tend to become institutionalized and resist change. But an independent action and research program specifically designed to pinpoint problems and remedies and to lay the basis for citizen-initiated critiques would be valuable insurance against institutional resistance.

Continuing community conference. Another device that might improve information and understanding in a new town is a "continuing community conference." Such a group, composed of officials and leaders of the community and neighborhoods, informed by the action and research program and assisted by specialists in various fields, could monitor the physical and political development of the new town and fashion proposals for further growth. The conference would be concerned with the social and political institutions of the new town, not solely with the narrow issues of governmental structure and public law.

The continuing community conference could also provide a place where citizens with different backgrounds and values could pool their ideas about how best to achieve their common goals. Through this means a body politic could be fostered, making up in some measure for the lack of civic experience and history in new towns.

Community foundation. A community foundation might be useful for stimulating and funding the wide range of high-risk but necessary voluntary and service activities that enrich a community but are difficult to start from scratch. A foundation could be free from the paternalism of either the government or the developer and could provide the initial working capital for such things as children's theater and preschool programs, teen-age centers, cultural programs and continuing education or community research efforts.

DIVERSITY: PRECONDITION FOR DEMOCRACY

From the first stages of settlement, new towns must have a diverse population and a broad range of economic and social activities. Development plans should recognize this objective as a precondition for democratic communities.

Federal requirements for population diversity as a condition of assistance will help reduce resistance to social balance in new towns. Moreover, many people who move into well-conceived new towns tend to regard social diversity as part of their purpose and civic spirit. The concept of an exciting new town can gain popular support because it also can meet critical community problems in an economic fashion. Where a total system is presented, including prospects for diversity and participation in development, the opportunity for both political and economic success can be substantially increased.

Planning for diversity entails a conscious effort to provide not only housing but jobs, services and amenities that will attract low-income as well as higher-income people. New towns must compete in the housing market for both classes of consumers. They can compete effectively with more homogeneous communities only by providing a higher level of amenities and services.

But the racial and economic integration of a new town can be an important marketable amenity. If towns are planned to include a diverse population and a pluralistic economy from the start, no single group will be guaranteed control of the initial governmental machinery and the power to exclude other groups.

To assure that new towns will be open to all races and ethnic groups at all income levels, neither the federal government nor the states can take a passive stance toward developers on the question of open communities. **Public agencies should insist on an affirmative planning strategy and marketing program that will increase the chances of achieving the objective of a "racially and economically balanced" community.** Federal and state officials should assist the developer by encouraging industrial location or modernization in all types of new towns and by providing support services, including subsidies if necessary, for programs that serve the public interest.

Title VII of the 1970 housing act encourages federal agencies to cooperate with one another in support of new-town development. State agencies—particularly those responsible for roads, education, sanitation, health, housing and parks—must follow a similar course. Their coordination in the funding of public activities can spell the difference between success and failure in the economic and social development of new towns. The agency responsible for state participation in their development needs the power to coordinate public works and services and to make sure that they are provided as the community is settled.

ROLE OF STATE AND LOCAL GOVERNMENTS

State and local governments, taking full advantage of Title VII of the Housing and Urban Development Act of 1970, must create the capability to plan and develop new towns either alone or in partnership with private developers. States should adopt imaginative legislation to assure that new towns realize their full potential for self-government.

In passing the 1970 act, Congress established the base for an effective new-town program. Now vigorous federal implementation of the legislation is required. By making federal assistance available to public agencies as well as to private developers in planning and developing new communities, Title VII encourages increased assistance and activity by state and local governments in the new-town movement.* Such activity can make it possible for the development of new towns to become a significant part of state and regional urban growth policies. Increasingly, states and their subdivisions should be participating financially in new towns, both directly as builders of them and indirectly through investments in the construction and provision of services and facilities.

Standards for State Activity

New towns are of such a nature that the public interest in them is substantial. As they become integral parts of state and national urban growth policy, they must reflect publicly determined standards. Existing state legislation and administrative procedures should be carefully reviewed with the aim of assuring responsible and effective governmental assistance in new-town development. Most states now have no policy what-

---

* Randy Hamilton comments: "This is not an unmixed blessing. While it is true that local governments under the terms of the federal legislation may participate in and sponsor new towns, it is also true that they cannot do so unless they waive a portion of their traditional immunity from federal income taxation. Municipal bonds issued for the purpose of building new towns under the 1970 housing act will not be tax exempt."

ever in this area, so model legislation should be prepared that will promote development of new towns and mobilize state resources for them.

Each state should define the role of new towns in its urban growth policies, set minimum standards for their development and establish procedures for protecting the public interest. The role of the state government itself—as developer, financier, expediter or regulator—must be defined. If public financial assistance is to be furnished, the state will have to commit its financial powers and its public agencies to make possible the infrastructure essential to successful new-town development. **Public policy must protect against the abuse of public credit and require that each new town contribute to the state's social and economic objectives. Private developers, for instance, should not be given public powers through control of special districts or other public corporations that might permit them to exploit bonding powers for their own interests.**

Access to Public Spaces and Facilities

Plans for new towns normally provide for extensive public spaces, facilities and services. Access to them must be determined in the planning phase and must be based on state and local needs. The notion that new towns serve only their residents is a very restrictive one, particularly if the towns are to be a conscious instrument of urban growth policies specifically designed to alleviate some of the ills of cities and suburbs. State and local development policies ought to establish guidelines for the use and control of new towns' resources and facilities to assure that all groups have access to public space and programs.

Encouraging Democratic Governance

New-town legislation in the states must establish policies and programs to provide democratic governance as an essential part of planning and development. Positive state policy is critical because state law regulates the creation and powers of local subdivisions. Without enlightened and strong state legislation, much that is recommended in this report cannot be attempted, much less achieved. Consequently, state policy must not merely permit but must actively encourage private developers and public agencies to experiment with programs to foster democratic practices in new towns. This effort will require a careful and comprehensive review of laws affecting both new-town development and the powers and organization of local governments.

The states should not prescribe rigid systems for new-town governance or participation. But they should require evidence of public participation in planning before granting permission to develop, and they should insist that developers, public and private, present positive and realistic programs for the involvement of citizens in new-town affairs. Plans should, of course, undergo a thorough and open public review prior to approval. The states should establish basic guidelines for membership and decision-making in homeowners' and community associations with the intent of making them genuinely democratic and not mere façades for continued corporate control of new-town affairs.

Flexibility in Governmental Forms

Encouraging experimentation requires the ability to distinguish between basic guarantees and procedural restrictions. **If a spirit of experimentation is to flourish, states must avoid the rigidity that characterizes most municipal legislation.** Specific forms of government should not be mandated by law or regulation. **Developers and local authorities should be given the latitude to explore a variety of approaches to urban democracy in new towns; alternative structures of government and participation should be encouraged.**

Present knowledge about what may be workable in specific circumstances is far too inadequate for the states to set limits on the form of government for new towns. Instead, the states should establish new-town review commissions with powers to approve a plan of government proposed for each new town as well as later alterations in it. Not only would such commissions serve as an expression of the public interest, but their members and staffs could also become a reservoir of knowledge and experience with different forms, powers and practices of self-government. They would then be an important resource for all local governments, new-town planners and citizens' groups seeking advice or technical assistance in creating or improving their governmental systems and political processes. The same body in each state might arbitrate boundary and jurisdictional issues concerning new towns and advise the governor and legislature on a broad range of intergovernmental problems affecting them, which might help to avoid such problems as competitive annexation proceedings and spiteful incorporations.

The states have much to gain from the new-town movement if they see in it an opportunity to test a wide range of new approaches to more effective and more democratic local government.

CONCLUSION

New-town democracy must evolve from experience. But that experience can come only if the problems of democracy are deliberately considered by everyone concerned with new-town planning and development. The new towns themselves are a prime testing ground and, in the pragmatic tradition of democracy, are destined to develop new approaches. It is vital to recognize the great potential of the new-town movement. It not only offers the promise of better living conditions; it also gives the citizen a better chance to participate in the governing of his community in an age of complex organization and esoteric technology.

For all its promise, the new-town movement will not resolve the many dilemmas of growth and decay of metropolitan areas. Nor is it the sole answer to problems of national resource allocation and conservation. Even a very large number of new towns will not do away with the pressing national problems posed by an inadequate housing supply, scarce and expensive health services, hostile race relations and maldistribution of incomes. So commitment to the new-town idea must not deflect resolution to deal with inner-city problems or with more general economic and social ills of our society. New towns, however, can and must be an important element in the achievement of broad national urban development goals. Properly conceived, new towns can be developed without imposing new social or economic costs on existing cities. More-over, they can help to alleviate urban social and economic problems. We believe that the new town can offer a higher level of social, economic and political equality and oppor-tunity than other forms of urban development. If their oppor-tunity is realized, the contribution of new towns to American life will be great.

BACKGROUND PAPER
by Royce Hanson

Introduction

For the first time in its history the United States is beginning to formulate national policy for urban growth. A central
feature of this emerging policy, affirmed by the Urban Growth
and New Community Development Act (Title VII of the
Housing and Urban Development Act of 1970), is support for
the creation of new towns—planned communities with diversified economies and populations and with facilities, services,
amenities and programs designed to provide both a healthier
and richer urban environment.

The focus of this paper is on the political institutions of
new towns, how they have developed to date and the issues
of democratic planning and development that will confront
urban policymakers, public and private, and new-town planners, developers and citizens as they attempt widespread
adaptation of the new-town concept to current American
needs.[2] Unless concern for the political mechanisms by which
new-town citizens will govern themselves is an integral part
of this attempt, it is unrealistic to assume that in the long run
new towns will fulfill their promise to provide effective alternatives to present patterns of urban living.

American history is replete with examples of new settlements created without prior thought to their form of government. As settlers moved westward during the nineteenth century, hundreds of towns sprang up. Though some were planned communities, they were not "new towns." Their plans were largely physical. In a few nineteenth century company towns some attempts were made to assure population and economic balance and to provide amenities and services in keeping with the standards of the time. But most towns grew suddenly, and, except for the few utopian settlements, there appears to have been little or no thought given to their political institutions.[3]

Local government was expected to take care of itself. And in one form or another, it did. In the great run of 1889, when Oklahoma Territory was opened for settlement, several towns were created instantly in areas designated for urban development, but no plans had been made for their governments. The formation of the government of Guthrie, the territorial capital, is illustrative of the informal methods used by the settlers to fill the governmental vacuum. Within twenty-four hours after the opening of the town to settlement, as disputes arose over claims to lots, criers called the people together to organize a provisional government. The settlers assembled, selected a committee on organization composed of one person from each state or territory represented at the meeting and, as their first act, repudiated the plat that had been drawn up as a map of the town. Nominations were made for mayor, and in the following two days of hotly disputed balloting several thousand voters participated. Tellers for the candidates could not agree on the count, so all candidates withdrew, and the settlers assembled once more and finally elected a mayor and a town council of seventeen members.[4]

The days of such spontaneous democracy are, for better or worse, past. Regardless of other considerations, the financial investment in new developments precludes leaving all governmental arrangements to informal assemblies of settlers. This does not mean that planning for local government has been an integral part of real estate development. On the contrary, as urban developments have mushroomed, altering population characteristics and political balance, they have been fitted into existing township, county and town governments, which have undergone gradual or cathartic—but almost always unplanned—changes. New subdivisions have been enfolded by annexation into existing municipalities or, as in Levittown, New Jersey and Park Forest, Illinois, distinct new communities have been incorporated, but their political structures have been based on existing governmental institutions with little change in basic laws or forms. This let-nature-take-its-course approach to political institutions may have been adequate for most large subdivisions with relatively homogeneous populations, but it has already proved inadequate for existing new towns. It will prove even more so for the many new towns with diverse populations and economies that will be built as a result of the impetus provided by the 1970 housing act.

Origin and Growth of the New-Towns Movement

EUROPEAN ORIGINS

The new-towns movement, now some three-quarters of a century old, had its origin in the intellectual rebellion against the dehumanizing environment of the drab, overcrowded industrial city. The movement's greatest prophet was Ebenezer Howard, whose *Garden Cities of Tomorrow* envisioned small, spacious communities linked together in a regional setting.[5] In time the idea ripened into a scheme for developing new towns, more spacious than the crowded big cities, with self-sufficient and balanced economies, where people could both live and work, start families and grow old.

A number of new towns were built or started before World War II. The movement did not get well under way, however, until the enactment of the New Towns Act in 1946. With this action, the British Government embarked on an ambitious program of constructing new towns to relieve overcrowding in London and other cities, to relocate industry, to reduce commuting needs and to save the countryside around major metropolitan areas from indiscriminate sprawl. New towns, surrounded by permanent greenbelts, were located at some distance from the central cities. To provide an employment base, inducements were offered to industries to relocate in the new towns. People who would work in the relocated industries were given housing preference. In the Scandinavian countries, particularly Sweden and Finland, satellite cities were built around the capitals, furthering both the ideas and techniques of new-town development. Today numerous European new towns demonstrate by their attractiveness, economy, convenience and social programs the advantages of these planned, relatively compact communities over conventional suburbs.

THE NEW-TOWNS MOVEMENT IN THE UNITED STATES

In the United States Lewis Mumford and Clarence Stein were among the early advocates of new towns.[6] For some years few people listened, but gradually many who were concerned with urban problems began to look at the new town as an "answer" to race and class segregation, automobile-dominated cities and land despoliation. Periodic proposals for federal assistance to develop new towns were opposed, however, by central city mayors, who saw new towns as draining off civic and business leaders, the industrial tax base, and federal funds, and by the building industry, which was far less industrialized than Europe's and contained many more small-scale builders, who opposed programs they viewed as suited only to huge housing or development companies.

The success of the European new towns and the gradual transformation of the building industry in the United States, combined with the continuing pressures of urban population and economic change, have made the idea of new towns progressively more acceptable. Regional plans proposing satellite cities as a major way of organizing growth began to appear in the early 1960s.[7] Title IV of the 1968 housing act provided for the first time effective federal financial guarantees for the developers of large-scale planned communities. Regarding existing programs of federal asssitance as inadequate to deal with projected urban growth, the National Committee on Urban Growth Policy in 1969 recommended establishment of 110 new cities in America by the year 2000—10 to be designed to house at least 1 million residents, the rest envisioned as satellites in existing urban regions with average populations of 100,000.[8]

While governments—particularly national governments—have been prime movers in new-town development abroad, new towns currently in various stages of development in the United States have been the work of private enterprise. The most notable of these are Reston, Virginia and Columbia, Maryland. By late 1970, however, the federal government, under Title IV of the 1968 housing act, had guaranteed loans to private developers for construction of three new communities in Minnesota, Illinois and Maryland.

The new-towns movement in the United States was finally recognized in a major way by enactment of Title VII of the Housing and Urban Development Act of 1970. This act represents a significant alteration in national attitudes toward urban growth. It outlines determinants for urban growth policy, including "encouraging planned, large-scale urban and new community development," and requires the President to submit a report to Congress on urban growth every two years. This act not only expands the federal loan guarantee program to private developers of new communities, but extends it to public agencies of state and local governments as well. A newly created federal Community Development Corporation, located in the Department of Housing and Urban Development, is empowered to guarantee loans for land assembly and development. Its assistance is not limited to the preliminary development stage, however. In order to minimize the financial burden incurred by public and private developers in the early stages of a new community's life, when investments are heavy and returns negligible, the secretary of HUD (through the Community Development Corporation) is authorized to grant to developers fifteen-year loans of up to $20 million each, to be applied to interest payments on loans originally taken out to permit development.

The Community Development Corporation may also make public service grants to state development agencies or other public bodies responsible for providing public services in a new community. These grants cover an initial period of development, up to three years, prior to completion of permanent servicing arrangements. They assure that new communities can be provided from the start with a level of services often lacking in conventional subdivision developments.

Supplementary federal grants of up to 20 percent of project cost are also made available in a large number of program areas to provide help and incentives for good design and protection of the environment. Finally, to help new communities in dealing with social and environmental problems, the secretary of HUD may provide technical assistance to both private and public developers and grants of up to two-thirds of the project planning cost.

Other parts of the act contain provisions for limited demonstration projects on federally owned land and for federal assistance to states for studies of urban growth policy.

State governments are also evincing increasing interest in new towns. In 1968 New York organized its Urban Development Corporation, which has plans in progress for several new towns. Other states are developing legislation either to facilitate new-town construction or to reduce any obstacles to it. Given the present surge of interest, by the end of this decade there may be a significant number of new towns under construction—many of them publicly funded, but most probably funded by a mixture of public and private investment.

Although the movement has its detractors and skeptics,[9] it appears to be one whose time has come. David Rockefeller, chairman of the Chase Manhattan Bank, for instance, recently urged creation of a $10 billion private fund to be used by the private sector for new towns. The question now is less whether new towns will be built than how and where.

Types of New Towns

As thinking about new towns has progressed, earlier, more rigid views of structure, size and distance from other urban settlements have yielded to more flexible and pragmatic approaches. Traditionally, a new town has been conceived as a *free-standing* development, planned to house a projected population of diverse economic classes and containing a wide range of economic activities and residential opportunities. It has been thought of as more heterogeneous and far more economically self-sufficient than a large conventional suburban development.

The feasibility of building such "frontier" new towns on an extensive scale depends on national policies that strongly encourage, or even compel, industrial relocation in order to provide an adequate economic base for them. In the absence of a national relocation program, it seems likely that in the United States far more emphasis will be placed on new towns developed as satellites of major metropolitan centers. These *satellite new towns,* while less economically self-sufficient and self-contained than traditional new towns, show greater immediate promise, for they offer an effective means of organizing the urban growth of existing metropolitan regions.

In recent years there has also been an increasing interest in the possibility of creating *new towns in-town,* compact sub-cities within the city, diverse in population and economy but not physically separated from surrounding urban areas.[10] New towns in-town can be developed on unused land or on land made available by urban redevelopment programs. Although no such communities have yet been developed in the United States, plans have been prepared for at least three—in the District of Columbia, on Welfare Island in New York City and near Toledo in Lucas County, Ohio. Others have been proposed for Minneapolis and Staten Island. One variation of this idea, suggested for the Detroit area, envisages the development of a "paired" new town. According to this scheme, one portion of the community would be situated in a downtown redevelopment area and the other in the suburbs. Though geographically separated, these two components would be linked through common social, economic and political systems.[11]

A fourth kind of American new town that may become important in state and national urban growth policies is the *add-on new town,* which uses an existing small town as the starting point for the development of a much larger new town. Such new towns can utilize existing infrastructure, thereby reducing some of the extensive "front-end" costs such as heavy investment in land improvements that are incurred by free-standing and satellite new towns before housing can be built and sold.

The new town in the United States, with its variety of forms, might be defined "as a matter of scale and process rather than by some of the conventional criteria which have identified the New Towns movement."[12] Certainly a new town must be a large-scale development whose size makes possible land and production economies, encouraging better and more varied uses of land and providing opportunities for diversity in population and in economic activities. But a genuine new town does more. It provides an alternative to the anomie, sterility and chaos in city and suburban life. It can be designed to reduce congestion and commuter travel; to house families of all income levels, including low-income families; to make available a variety of community services; and to offer the amenities of urban civilization. The new town, in short, is a comprehensive development that is planned consciously to broaden social and economic choice and opportunity.

Few existing large-scale developments in the United States can be considered new towns. In fact, the greatest threat to the new-towns movement is the tendency for every planned residential development to be advertised as a "new town" or "new-town sector," whether or not it offers the diversity of economic and social opportunity essential for a new town. The idea that a city is a system in which the many parts and activities are interdependent is basic to the development processes of a new town. Innovations in design and programs based on this idea are therefore requisites for a genuine new town, whether free-standing, satellite, in-town or added-on to an old town. A new town is more than a large development that provides a better place to live. That alone would be an improvement over much contemporary urban development, but the new town, as it has developed historically, holds out hope for a better way of life as well. To fulfill this hope, it must promote democratic practices in decision-making and social relations.

The Current Governance of New Towns

Because new towns are more comprehensively planned than conventional developments, consideration of social and political institutions can be an important aspect of their planning and development. But unfortunately governmental arrangements for new towns have to date been thought of almost exclusively in relation to problems of land acquisition, finance and organization of development agencies and the provision of service to new-town residents.

Most local governments in the United States are inadequate to the tasks which confront them. This is especially true of county governments, on which most new towns will have to rely for their initial services. Even in states with a strong county home rule tradition, urban counties are now faced with many of the same problems that have demoralized cities. Many are so big that officials and offices are remote from citizens and are politically nebulous for most voters, especially new residents. Governmental structure is often antiquated and many governments are poorly staffed and managed. Responsibility for services is fragmented among a wide variety of agencies, making coordinated delivery of services to a new town a near impossibility.

The early years of development may also place a heavy fiscal strain on the county or other "parent" jurisdiction in which the new town is to be located. A rural county, for instance, not infrequently will lack the revenue necessary to provide the public improvements—roads, schools, sanitary facilities—needed in the initial stages of development before tax-paying industries arrive to expand the tax base. The fiscal strain can create a political crisis detrimental to the future of the new community as the taxes of older residents escalate to provide services for the new-town residents, who are not yet a major political power in the jurisdiction. On the other hand, sole reliance on the undeveloped new town's tax base can create severe problems in marketing bonds or debt service and can produce a debt structure that makes development prohibitive. Even a modern, urbanized county or a major city will probably already face such serious fiscal problems that it cannot politically afford heavy investment in the initial construction and service costs of a new town, let alone provide newcomers a higher level of services than that given other taxpayers. If public financing of capital improvements is not available, the private developer may have to incur these initial costs. This may create problems of cash flow for the developer. It may also put the local government in a position of relying on the developer to provide public improvements, though it has few means of holding him accountable for his performance.[13]

It is in this setting that most new-town development has taken place. As development has progressed, the officials of the parent jurisdiction and its citizens, the developer and the residents of the new town, whose interests often conflict, have attempted to fit the new town into the existing governmental framework and to improvise means of serving and governing it.

If a new town is to succeed, steps must be taken from its inception to assure financing and administering of its amenities, facilities and services at a level clearly above that of surrounding areas, where community services are often provided at marginal levels. Ultimately there must be some means whereby control over these public community services can be exercised by the people who pay for and use them. These two needs cannot always be met by the same arrangement at the same time. New towns have used a variety of approaches, each of which illuminates some of the problems of fostering democratic self-government in new towns.

CORPORATE GOVERNMENT: THE DEVELOPER

The established pattern of American new-town development has been for a development corporation to assemble the land with no help from, and probably without the knowledge of, local or state governments and to arrange financing entirely through the private money market.[14] The local authority is then petitioned for approval of the master plan and for appropriate zoning, which are subject to the usual political influences, which are either in support of or in opposition to the developer's plans and which are largely those the developer and citizens already living in the jurisdiction of the proposed new town can bring to bear.

When the first houses are ready for occupancy and people move in, they find themselves, as do most suburbanites, dealing with their developer as well as the local government. Unless the developer or these early residents incorporate or make some other provision for the new town's government, there is no official mechanism for citizen participation. New-town citizens as such have no direct control over the remaining development and therefore have no official power in dealing with the developer. Homeowners' associations or other types of community organizations that may be formed must compete with the developer and with any other organizations in the jurisdiction for influence with the parent local government. Until development is largely completed, however, the developer is the key figure in the political system: as owner of the undeveloped land, he has the initiative in dealing with the local government, which has a financial interest in continued development. As a consequence the developer is in a strong position to bargain for public services for his development and to act as intermediary between the new-town residents and the government. His political position is enhanced by the fact that home values depend in part on his ability to complete his plan, so he often has the active cooperation of residents in dealing with the local government.

In the initial stages of development the developer is primarily responsible for providing public services and amenities. In most instances he is responsible for construction of streets and, often, for the provision of water and sewage facilities. He may provide rudimentary police and fire services if the local government cannot do so. He will set aside spaces for public schools and parks. He is also, of course, the source of a large number of private services such as drainage and landscaping of private lots. He may place his stamp not only on the architecture but on cultural and recreational programs, endowing some activities, subsidizing others and showing no interest in still others. He may retain a golf course as a private, profit-making activity or turn a lake, park, walkway or bike trail over to a homeowners' or community association, which will usually be controlled by him until development and occupancy are well advanced. The power of the developer to dispose of parks and open spaces or to control the use of them offers an opportunity for abuse without public accountability unless the parent jurisdiction provides for public regulation of parks and other public areas and facilities in its zoning or other laws. The basic approach to new-town government that has developed from this relationship might best be described as benevolent despotism by the developer, the degrees of benevolence and despotism varying with the corporation concerned.

PRIVATE GOVERNMENT: THE HOMEOWNERS' OR COMMUNITY ASSOCIATION

A private government through a homeowners' or community association is often established by the developer to assure that the amenities he provides will be maintained by the residents and to shift the financial burden of maintaining these amenities from himself to the residents. Membership in a homeowners' association is usually covenanted with the land. Every home buyer automatically becomes a member of the association and liable for its dues or assessments. The homeowners' association normally bears responsibility for the maintenance of common areas and facilities deeded to it by the developer. It is funded through assessments of property owners.

Radburn, New Jersey

A prototype for homeowners' associations was created in Radburn, New Jersey, in the later 1920s.[15] Radburn's planners wanted to assure that they would be successful in completing their planned community. Louis Brownlow, who greatly influenced the governmental arrangements, also wanted a vehicle for democratic participation ready when the first residents moved in.[16] The device used to merge these objectives was the "Radburn Restrictions,"[17] covenants under which the Radburn Protective Restrictions and Community Association became a legal entity before the first conveyance of a home to a purchaser. Within this legal structure the Radburn Association was created with a board of nine members, five representing the developer. Four were "public interest" trustees, citizens of northern New Jersey interested in community planning.

Board members were elected at annual meetings for overlapping three-year terms. As corporation officials and public interest trustees resigned for various reasons, the remaining trustees elected Radburn residents to succeed them, so that the number of resident trustees gradually increased until, in 1948, no spokesman for the corporation remained on the board.

The Radburn Association demonstrated that a community association could enforce a scheme of restrictions against all owners and tenants in a community. The association operated as a private government through which residents participated in its limited functions. They were also voters and taxpayers of the borough of Fair Lawn and of Bergen County, competing with citizens of neighboring areas for the services of these public governments. In the early years the Radburn Association maintained a higher level of local services than the public agencies provided. For instance, the association paid a tuition supplement to a high school in another jurisdiction because its members preferred to send their children to a better school than the one which they would otherwise have attended. By 1964 the quality of most municipal services in Fair Lawn had caught up with services in Radburn, and the association's main function was to conduct recreational programs and maintain the areas it owned.

The Radburn experience in the establishment of automatic homeowners' associations has been repeated in a number of large subdivisions and planned community developments. Reston, Virginia has a variation of this type of association.

Reston, Virginia

The first two villages built in Reston had covenanted, automatic homeowners' associations based essentially on the Radburn model. At the initiative of the developer, who sought a unified mechanism for providing community services and a single organization for dealing with residents, these associations were merged in 1970 over the strident objections of some members. Most opposition came from the Second Association, which served the area in which traditional homes had been built. Some citizens in this area, which is remote from the first village center, did not share the "activist" values of the First Association and opposed the added costs of a merged association.

All property owners are members of the Reston Homeowners' Association. Each housing unit has one vote, and the developer retains a vote for each unsold unit. He is thus assured of majority control of the directors until over half the units are sold and in any event will have at least a third of all membership votes until 1985. The members of the association annually elect three of the nine directors, who serve three-year, overlapping terms.

The association operates and maintains swimming pools, tennis courts, playgrounds, ball fields, walkways and open spaces that have been conveyed to it by the developer. In addition, the association operates an architectural review board, consisting of six architects and two laymen, which must approve all new structures and exterior alterations to existing property. The developer chooses all the members except one architect and one layman. Since 1969 the association has employed a full-time executive director.

To broaden participation in the affairs of the association, a town council was established as an advisory body to the homeowners' association in the 1970 merger. Renters may vote in the council, as may all adult members of a household. The developer has no votes in the council, but the directors still exercise all legal power over association affairs and the majority of directorships is retained by the developer.

Townhouse owners in Reston automatically belong to "cluster associations" (so called because the townhouses are built in clusters) in addition to the homeowners' association. Membership in each cluster association is on the basis of property ownership, with the developer voting the unsold lots plus one vote. The cluster associations maintain the common property of the cluster and are responsible for services such as upkeep of landscaped areas, sidewalks, outdoor lighting and parking areas, removal of snow and maintenance of playgrounds. A Restonian who lives in a townhouse pays dues to both the cluster and the homeowners' associations in addition to his local taxes, which pay for the county's usual services.

Columbia, Maryland

The basic pattern of private government in Columbia, in Howard County, Maryland, is quite different from that of Reston. The Columbia Park and Recreation Association (The Columbia Association) is organized as a private corporation with a very broad charter. It may undertake almost any function not prohibited by law that its board of directors desires. The association was formed before the new town was opened to residents, and a professional manager was appointed to administer its affairs.

The original board consisted of seven appointees of the developer. For each four thousand units of housing that are occupied (whether owned or rented), one Columbia resident will be added to the board of directors. Beginning in 1976, one of the directors representing the developer will be dropped from the board annually until 1980, when the terms of the last three will expire simultaneously. The resident directors are appointed by the board but nominated by the Columbia Council, which consists of one representative from each "village" in the new town. The council representatives are elected by secret ballot in each village, which also elects a five-member board for its village association. One vote is cast by the occupants of each dwelling unit, whether renters or owners. Owners of multiunit buildings have only one vote. The village boards are advisory to the Columbia Association board.

The Columbia Association has a wide range of functions, including construction and maintenance of community facilities such as community centers and swimming pools; conduct of recreation programs, an early childhood education program and an information and complaint service; and administration of a community transportation program in the new town.

One of the unique features of the Columbia Association is that it assesses businesses as well as residential property to support activities, thus easing the burden on homeowners. The association's assessment of property owners is based on the property values established by the Howard County Assessor. Additional fees are charged for use of facilities such as swimming pools.

Not all the open space in Columbia will remain under the jurisdiction of the Columbia Association; 50 percent is to be retained as public areas by Howard County. Some of the association's facilities such as swimming pools and skating rinks are also open to the general public on a fee basis.

Problems of Governance Through Associations

A homeowners' or community association offers some obvious advantages to the developer and to the home buyer. If votes in the governing body are based on site ownership or occupancy, the developer will have majority control until the development is more than half sold, and thus he can be assured of substantial completion of the development on the basis of plans in which he has a very large financial investment. In the meantime the developer is able, through the association's assessment system, to relieve himself of costly maintenance programs by deeding many common facilities to the homeowners. Unless the developer suffers financial collapse or alters course while he still holds the majority of votes in the association, the home buyer has reasonable assurance that the association will protect his investment in a planned community by maintaining common areas and amenities and even.

43

in some cases, by assessing derelict owners for improvements if individual acts of neglect affect the appearance of the community. In return, the homeowner pays assessments or "dues" to the cluster or village association and to the community association in addition to his mortgage payments and local property taxes.

The local government may also benefit from the development and maintenance by the association of parks and community programs without use of local revenue. This may mean, however, that so-called public areas are in fact private property unless, as in Columbia, the parent government in its zoning ordinances requires public retention of some open space in the plan.

Along with the advantages, the use of the private association as the principal, or sole, vehicle of new-town governance gives rise to a number of problems, the most serious of which have been described by Stanley Scott.[18] One of these problems involves a feature of the new town that makes it most inviting as a place to live—its parks and open spaces and community facilities. The by-passing of local governments by the developer's assignment of major community open space and facilities to homeowners' associations can raise questions of the public interest if steps are not taken to assure public access to these community areas. One might quibble very little over assignment to a community association of a parking lot or common green in a townhouse cluster or garden apartment area, but one might question such exclusive use of a neighborhood park, a major nature area, a lake or a walkway, since many area residents outside the new town may wish to use them. But to transfer all of these to the local government might be equally unsatisfactory. A rural county or township in which a new town is located may not be equipped to develop such areas or to administer them, at least to satisfactory standards, and the new-town residents would lack a park system and community facilities because of the government's inability or unwillingness to provide them.

Another problem discussed by Scott is that many homeowners' associations, because of dominance by upper- and middle-income residents, tend to institutionalize community or neighborhood segregation. They may view membership by residents of apartments as "a problem" and may even resist the introduction of low-income housing in the new town. In addition, the developer has enormous control over the character of the association not only because he generally maintains voting control of it for some time but because, before the first resident moves in, he can determine its structure through provisions for association membership, covenanted by him with the land. If, for example, the developer decides that the owner rather than the tenants should cast the votes of a multiunit dwelling, the problems of representativeness are exacerbated, since the notion that only freeholders should have suffrage in local elections is built into the association.

Some critics of such inequities suggest that under these circumstances the use of a homeowner's association to perform governmental or quasi-governmental functions, especially levying assessments that presumably are reflected in rents, may violate the Fourteenth Amendment to the Constitution, which guarantees to all citizens equal protection of the laws. The question is whether, in spite of their private character, homeowners' or community associations are so similar to municipal corporations in the things they do that renters, spouses and other adult members of a family who are unable to vote are denied equal representation in their local "government."[19]

In new towns with diversified populations, where thought has been given to democratic participation of residents in new-town affairs in the planning and development stage, the problem of upper-income bias in homeowners' associations can be mitigated. For example, the Columbia Association's provision for basing voting on dwelling units rather than on ownership suggests one way of making new-town associations more representative. But Columbia's limitation of one vote per dwelling unit may reduce the influence of low-income residents, who are more likely than upper-income residents to have children of voting age and other adult relatives living with the family.

Size is one of the most formidable practical problems for the homeowners' or community associations. This has led Scott to suggest that they may be suitable only for small groups of residents rather than for the large populations envisioned for new towns. But the village or cluster association which serves a small, compact group of homes often lacks the necessary management capacity and is too small to provide services economically to its members without unreasonably high assessments. A growing number of Reston citizens seem to be coming to this conclusion. Pooling funds and staff or merging into a single organization embracing the entire new town may be the only solution to these problems.

But as experience since the 1970 merger of the two Reston homeowners' associations indicates, the differences between communities in the same new town may impede the functioning of a merged association, especially if the association members from one community view the role of the association in a more "private" than public sense while the members from another community tend toward the opposite view. High-income residents may look on the association as a club serving its members. Renters and low-income residents may see the association more as a local quasi-government which should continue to expand its public services to a wider range of citizens. When these two groups of residents are physically separated, as they are in most new towns, placing them both in the same association produces conflict with which an association controlled by the developer and limited by its covenants to narrow concerns is not very well equipped to cope.

Associations are essentially private in form and character, even if they have voting provisions based on the principle of one man, one vote. They are bodies corporate but not politic. They may, in some form, be very desirable as one of several instruments of government, but it is questionable whether they should be the principal or permanent means of public participation in new-town affairs. At best they seem fragile instruments for expression of the public interest, since they clearly represent some interests and limit participation by others. They nonetheless suggest the kind of governmental arrangements that may be made where existing public institutions are unable or unwilling to provide the services and amenities essential to a new town. They appear to serve admirably for some aspects of new community governance in the early stages of development but seem less suited politically, fiscally and managerially for even the same tasks by the time the community reaches a population of 25,000, 50,000 or

100,000. At such levels of population serious questions may also be raised about the division of labor between the private and public sectors of the government.

A homeowners' or community association, with its limited functions, is not, of course, an official government. Every new town is under the jurisdiction of one or more governmental subdivisions—the state, the county and/or the city or township and, often, a number of special purpose districts. The town may also incorporate as a municipality and establish a government of its own or be designated a special district.

Unincorporated New Towns: Reston and Columbia

Most new towns are unincorporated and depend on their county governments and their developers for local services. The kinds of governmental relationships that new towns in this situation have developed in order to secure the levels of amenities and services promised in their development plans are illustrated by the experience of Reston and Columbia, located in quite different kinds of counties.

Reston is in Fairfax County, Virginia, one of the nation's most rapidly growing areas. In Virginia, cities and counties are completely separated, so urban counties provide all municipal services. Since 1950 Fairfax County has had a strong urban government and has successfully fought off annexation attempts by cities, in part because county services have been as good as or better than those furnished by the cities. Fairfax County's governing Board of Supervisors is elected from single-member districts, and because of its size Reston has an important voice in its district and will eventually dominate it.

The incorporation of Reston and its consequent organization as a separate political subdivision has never been seriously considered, and it is not likely to be, especially since recent state legislation prohibits new incorporations in urban counties. The basic reason for this legislation is that in Virginia land inside cities cannot be taxed by the surrounding county government. If Reston had incorporated, the county, having zoned the land for a new town and provided initial services, would subsequently have lost all the revenue generated by its actions when Reston became eligible, through population growth, for city status.

Reston, then, must compete with all other communities in Fairfax County for county services. As a "showcase" community it has fared quite well in this competition. The county has been cooperative in building elementary schools and in providing other services, and the level of public services in the county at large is sufficiently high that there are no marked differences between Reston and other communities. Because of its tax base, the county has been able to absorb the cost of the public investments in the new town without material change in the overall tax rate.

Columbia, also unincorporated, depends on Howard County, Maryland, for many services. Howard County, in contrast to Fairfax, is an exurban-rural county. Until Columbia was built it had a population of less than 50,000. Howard County has had an enlightened public leadership that has responded favorably to the new town, and the formerly rural county government has been converted into a much more urban-oriented one. A new charter providing for broad home rule powers and an elected chief executive has been adopted. The Columbia Association, however, had to provide many of the initial services and amenities planned for the new town, since the county could not have provided them without a politically disastrous impact on its tax rate. If development proceeds as planned Columbia will eventually dominate the county. But its population is not yet large enough to give it a commanding position in the county council, which, in accordance with Maryland law, is elected at large. Some opposition to the further development of Columbia began to appear in county politics in 1970, although it seems clear that Columbia's fiscal impact on Howard County has been highly beneficial, generating more revenues than expenditures.

While the county governments have tended to protect the developers of both Reston and Columbia and their initial plans, and while the homeowners' or community associations have provided a quasi-public vehicle for the political organization of these towns, in their general political development they do not appear to have departed substantially from the character and style of typical suburban subdivision politics. The intensity of political activity may be somewhat greater, but the same newcomer–old resident political battle that has characterized suburban development of hitherto rural counties appears to be brewing in Howard County. It is unlikely that the incorporation of Columbia as a city would appreciably reduce this conflict.

Given the strong county systems in Maryland and Virginia, incorporation would apparently not have benefited either Reston or Columbia on financial grounds or in terms of political accommodation. Howard County had difficulties in providing initial services at the standards of adequacy held by Columbia's developer and residents. But both Howard and Fairfax counties have probably been better equipped to provide services than newly incorporated but only partially developed new towns would have been. Assimilation into the total fabric of county politics has not only eased the fiscal burden on the new-town residents but has facilitated their adjustment to the local political system. The homeowners' or community associations, citizens' associations, and a variety of other voluntary organizations have provided channels for a high level of participation in community affairs.

Incorporation and Annexation

New towns, of course, can incorporate in most states as an alternative to depending on county governments for public services and as focal points for local political organization. Some students of the political development of new towns insist that the sooner one incorporates the better.[20] Incorporation as an independent municipality certainly provides a sense of identity and helps to stimulate new-town community spirit. It can also protect the developer from an inept county government or from annexation by a city that is set on gaining revenue but that has little interest in providing the level of services needed to make the new town marketable. A municipality can issue bonds and receive federal grants-in-aid and state equalization grants and shared revenues. It can provide police and other services and can carry out regulatory functions that cannot be performed by homeowners' or community associations. A municipality often has an independent school system as well.

Some of these advantages may be offset by the limitations certain states place on municipal debt and tax rates, which virtually prevent operation above a subsistence level. Furthermore, homeowners' or community associations based on restrictive covenants may be more effective than public agencies in enforcing esthetic standards and environmental restrictions. Also some community services and amenities of new towns such as preschools, swimming pools and arts programs are not considered appropriate municipal functions in some states.

The proposed "new city" of Irvine, California illustrates the importance and the problems of incorporation, although some question may be raised as to whether it is a new town as that term has been defined here. Irvine, planned to house over 400,000 people when complete, will eventually include all of what is now called "the Irvine Ranch," originally a very large unincorporated area within a single county but within annexation reach of at least five municipalities. Any part of the area that remains unincorporated is threatened with annexation by the neighboring municipalities. If the whole area prematurely incorporated as a new city, its initially small population would have to assume responsibility for the development of a much larger area. One alternative, apparently favored by both the citizens and the developer, is to incorporate the currently built-up area and to try to fight off annexation of the rest of the area by neighboring cities. Then, as development proceeds under the jurisdiction of Orange County, the new city will annex the newly developed areas. If an area is populated before it annexed, the question of annexation will be decided by concurrent referenda in that area and in the municipality seeking to annex it.

The problem for many new towns will be not whether to incorporate but when to do it. Early incorporation can give the first residents great power over future development if their quarrels with the developer result in his being forced by the parent government to alter the development plan. Experience indicates, however, that the developer has relatively little to fear for his overall plan, although his practices may be the focus of substantial political cleavage. In his studies of Levittown, New Jersey and Park Forest, Illinois, Herbert Gans points out that municipal problems so occupied the parent governments that there was little time for them to consider private complaints against the developers, who maintained good rapport with the local governments.[21] Furthermore, one of the interesting aspects of citizen-developer relations in Reston and Columbia is that the citizens often seem to be more avid supporters of the original plans than the developers. Reston's developer, the Gulf-Reston Corporation, has constantly had to convince the citizenry that its proposed alterations in the plan do not represent an abandonment of "new-town principles."

Special Districts

Special districts have been used as interim governmental devices for new towns. Perhaps the best known of these is the Estero Improvement District, created in 1960 to provide municipal services for Foster City, California. The developer was permitted to appoint the entire board of the Estero District, and it was not subject to public control by either the county or the state government. The developer, a private corporation, was thus able to finance capital improvements in its own development by using public power to issue bonds. Over the years, many municipalities have made decisions that directly benefited private interests. There is a vital distinction, however, between the issuance of bonds that benefit a single corporation by an elected city council or a publicly appointed board and empowering that corporation to use public credit itself, without subsequent electoral accountability. The potential for abuse in the latter arrangement is quite obvious. Foster City raises, in sharp relief, the problem of reconciling the interests of the developer, the residents and the broader public of the county and state.

Experience with the Estero District and the similar Embarcadero Municipal Improvement District (which was the center of a major scandal over diversion of public funds to private use) resulted in changes in California law concerning the use of such districts to protect better the public interest and credit. But the lessons seem not to have reached beyond California. Arizona, for instance, recently enacted legislation which will permit practices similar to the ones that California has now prohibited.

Single-purpose districts, which permit the use of public credit for such purposes as providing water and reclaiming land, are commonly employed in many parts of the country. They are established when fiscal problems such as marketing bonds or debt service have not been adequately anticipated. In such a case, providing the necessary services by increasing the public debt through the usual financial processes would so affect the tax rate as to impede development rather than facilitate it. However, special districts, whether single or multipurpose, tend to remove some governmental functions from surveillance by the electorate. Redwood City, California, seems to have overcome this problem through the use of the dependent district. There, the improvement district area, Redwood Shores, was annexed to Redwood City. The city council serves as the board of the improvement district, and thus the district is legally and administratively an arm of an existing city government.

New Towns in Overlapping Jurisdictions

As more new towns are planned, they may be confronted with the problem of whether to remain under the jurisdiction of the county government, to incorporate or to be annexed by a municipality. There are already a number of new towns being planned whose boundaries will overlap several existing county or municipal jurisdictions. This situation can further complicate the problems of governmental relationships for both the new town and for the governmental jurisdictions concerned.

In California counties, proposed incorporations and annexations are subject to approval by local agency formation commissions (LAFCs). Operating on a county basis, the LAFCs appear to have prevented some of the most flagrant abuses of special districts and of premature annexations and incorporations, but the LAFC in Orange County was unable to find a suitable means of resolving the threatened annexation problems of Irvine. Furthermore, the number of special districts in California has actually increased since the LAFCs have been in operation. In light of this experience some states may have to take jurisdiction over organizing governments for new towns whose boundaries cut across county lines or whose impact on a neighboring county or city is substantial.

Issues in Democratic Development of New Towns

The process of planning and development of most new towns in both Europe and the United States has been fairly autocratic. Even the state and local jurisdictions embracing the new towns have participated very little in design beyond exercising their legal powers to approve proposals by developers. The few public bodies actively engaged in planning new communities have viewed their task as the solution of engineering and fiscal problems, not as the fostering of democratic participation. Those who want to "get on with it" approach new-town development very much like any large construction problem, except that there is a tendency to be even more autocratic than in developing ordinary subdivisions—to seek power to develop without review or control by local authorities, and in some cases even to overturn local land use policies which tend to frustrate the attainment of the social objectives of new towns.

The developer, whether public or private, may well fear that a plan subject to all the trials of democratic processes may be impossible to carry out, given the time-cost factors and the difficulties of achieving the necessary rationality and balance of land uses. He may also fear that too much "democracy" during development may make it impossible for him to implement a well-drawn plan, especially if the wishes of the first residents conflict with a plan approved before they were there. This fear accounts for the reluctance of some new-town developers to encourage early municipal incorporation, which might result in the residents' acquiring public planning and zoning powers that could upset the financial position of the developer.

Social innovation is not necessarily incompatible with participation by ordinary citizens in decision-making. The social or physical planner often complains that he is driven by citizens toward the commonplace solution or design. While citizen participation or control is by no means a guarantee of innovation, there is not much evidence that either private or public bureaucracies are bursting with new ideas. Citizen control can retard development, but so can a sense of alienation by citizens or interminable bureaucratic review and control. If the need for both creativity and public accountability is to be met, the process of new-town development demands better management of the tensions between the developers, the professionals, their clients and local governments.

From the standpoint of development alone, the new town's governmental system is crucial. Initial design has great influence on the success of a new town, but the crucial test is how the residents actually interact, not how it is supposed they will live. Human behavior is not constant over time. Tastes and manners change. The character of housing demand may alter during the several years spanned by the development process. Some means of feeding back the reactions of early residents to improve the next increment of development is essential. While market surveys can reveal some useful information for replanning, they cannot be employed as a substitute for spontaneous expression of residents' desires. Any new settlement gives rise to political activity that results in pressures on the developer such as demands for services or opposition to plan alterations or the carrying out of new phases of an already approved plan. The ways in which the desires of the residents of a new town are expressed are of concern to the developer and to parent state and local governments.

In light of this, it is surprising that so little thought has been given to governmental arrangements and processes. The ideology of planning, especially of new towns, suggests that environment is a major factor in social behavior and may also condition political behavior. It is possible to design certain physical aspects of a new town so as to encourage political communication. The arrangement and internal configuration of neighborhoods, economic stratification in residential price structure, marketing strategies for land, advertising, land sales and job recruiting all have an impact on the characteristics of the new town and consequently on its constituency and politics.

The size of political bodies, the scale of constituencies and geographic units of participation also affect who participates in what, and to what effect. Much thought has gone into neighborhoods, churches, shopping centers, schools and child care facilities, but relatively little into the possibilities for neighborhood politics and the political linkages between the neighborhood and the metropolis or state.

All of this suggests that attempts to reconcile the conflicts between the interests of developers and citizens should begin in the early stages of new-town planning. It also suggests that governmental planners need to be aware of the role that new towns may play in developing more effective democratic institutions and processes.

From this perspective, the involvement of citizens in the economic, social and political aspects of the planning process might conceivably be used as an instrument of democratic development, in spite of the complex and often conflicting interests involved in new-town planning and development. This conclusion assumes that popular experience in the process of development is basic to creation of the public intelligence necessary to master the urban environment.

Existing governmental arrangements for new towns, whether public or private, generally have been predicated on the need for development financing and a high level of community services. Provision of a means for effective expression of citizen interests and public choices has tended, at best, to be a secondary consideration. But these towns offer an unequaled opportunity to test the effectiveness of democratic practices that established local governments have long neglected or never tried and that cannot be tested by imposing established governmental forms on the new towns. The need for basic local democracy matches or even transcends the need for institutions capable of funding and delivering services.

CONVERTING RESIDENTS INTO CITIZENS

Local self-government is not strictly necessary to provide services. Administrative divisions of larger governmental units could do this. But one of the most important functions of local government is to convert residents into citizens by affording them the opportunity to acquire civic experience through participation in governing, through sharing responsibility for public decisions. Local self-government also legitimates authority. Citizen participation in local decision-making inevitably influences the character of services and helps to determine the beneficiaries of government programs. In this way, authority is tempered and obligated to respond to local opinion.

Democratic Rituals versus Democratic Participation

Neither central city nor suburban governments now afford an adequate civic experience. They restrict the meaningful political participation from which such experience is gained, and they are poorly designed to manage conflict. Most local governments were organized for administrative housekeeping. They are based on politically antiseptic assumptions of human behavior and are equipped to deal with routine matters, not major questions of public policy. Even a decade of urban unrest has scarcely dented popular belief in the bland assumptions on which these governments are based. The homogeneity of suburban enclaves often excludes from consideration major problems that involve serious public conflicts. Small suburban governments lack jurisdiction over matters of substantial interest such as transportation; they have no political reason to be concerned with such problems as low-income housing because no group with a direct stake in it lives in their jurisdictions. In such circumstances, local government may educate citizens in democratic rituals, but it is ill equipped to give them meaningful experience in dealing with the issues of urban life that transcend localities.

57

A different set of circumstances limits the civic function of big-city governments, though they have diverse interests to deal with and are confronted with the most difficult public problems. Not only does their scale discourage broad participation, especially that of low-income groups and minorities, but representation is structured to allow a particular group, party or official bureaucracy to maintain control of political processes. As a result, the inertia of city governments favors those groups most interested in the status quo, who find the political system congenial and who have the time, money and skill required to overcome, or use for their own ends, its impediments. The private sector's urban institutions—voluntary agencies, united funds, hospitals, the bar and other professional organizations, public service unions and associations and organized citywide groups—follow the same pattern. Few cities have a self-conscious "power elite," but the political systems of all cities tend to be regulated by the interests that already have a foothold in some area of public policy.

Attempts have been made under the antipoverty and model cities programs to increase participation and to reduce city government to a manageable political scale. Neighborhood boards, corporations and committees run redevelopment programs, schools and model cities programs. Some of these have shown results in terms of both participation and improvements in service,[22] but they have focused on a rather narrow range of governmental problems. In most cases the right to make mistakes has been retained by the central organs rather than decentralized.

The Problem of Competence

Modern urban conditions place new demands on citizenship. Public decisions are increasingly made on the basis of considerable research and technical advice. For the citizen this means that a patriotic determination to participate is hardly sufficient if he hopes to be effective in dealing with large organizations or complex and technical problems—pollution control, community health and highway location, for example. Public pressure is no longer enough. That pressure must be sharply focused on the technical aspects of a problem.

Even citizens who are well trained may have substantial difficulty in translating their private knowledge and skills into effective participation in public affairs. Moreover, the level of information available to citizens is generally poor and poorly presented. Democratic development therefore involves more than merely making the opportunity for participation available through the usual channels. New towns will need to fashion processes that permit translation of private skills, information needs and perceptions into effective public participation in order to make citizens more independent of bureaucratic spoon-feeding and more competent to deal with public issues and officials.

The Problem of Managing Conflict

Participation in public life is undoubtedly specialized, in that few people participate in all matters. One of the standard stratagems of politics is for specialists in one area—schools, sewers, or planning—to create their own spheres of influence, buttressed by independent official agencies. When this strategy is successful, government becomes a cluster of clientele agencies. It works beautifully for those who agree with what is being done. By limiting access, conflict can be minimized. Each functional interest conducts its affairs somewhat independently of the others in a live-and-let-live atmosphere. There is really little competition for public resources except at the margins of program expansion. Where conflict is restricted, public knowledge is limited and the incentives to participate are reduced. The creation of agencies that carry out only specialized or a narrow range of activities cannot be expected to stimulate a high degree of citizen interest.

This suggests that if the objective is to develop broad participation in new-town affairs, the governmental system should acknowledge the existence of different interests in public policy and use the resulting political competition as a resource for strengthening democratic politics. This, in turn, argues for a general framework of government in which specialized groups will have to compete openly with each other for resources and power.

From the point of view of democratic development, general—as opposed to specialized—governmental responsibility teaches values of compromise, coalition, accommodation and tolerance, since competing interests must be reconciled in order to make decisions and allocate resources. The greater the diversity of activities, the more likely that competition for public resources and decisions will generate conflict. Conflict attracts attention and converts spectators into participants. Increased participation injects new and different interests into the political arena, requires development of experience and skills in conflict management and encourages more responsible performance by officials.

CITIZEN RESPONSIBILITY IN PLANNING AND DEVELOPMENT

Participation in all phases of new-town development can be anticipated and provided for from the beginning rather than being grafted onto a possibly hostile system as an afterthought or as a concession to pressures. The objective is to cultivate competent citizenship that identifies with the new town and shares public responsibility for its development both before it is built and after it has been inhabited. Because the development of the town is perceived as being in the public interest and because it affects a large segment of the population, it has a chance of engaging more citizens than do projects which are more limited in scope.

Public participation in new-town planning has heretofore been restricted to the elected representatives, appointed officials and interest groups of the parent government. This participation has been superficial in some cases and extensive and searching in others, depending on the amount of conflict and interest generated by the new-town proposal. Citizens of the parent jurisdiction have a substantial interest in a new town, for it will affect their tax rates, patterns of land use, the availability of community facilities, traffic patterns and school needs. While these interests must be recognized, especially in the earlier stages of development, the people coming to live in the new town will demand an increasing voice in the growth of their community and will tend to resent being governed by those who live outside it.

Future citizens of new towns are usually absent from the

initial planning process, for it is assumed that they cannot be identified. It may be relatively easy, however, to deduce a great deal about potential residents. For example, an in-town redevelopment effort may be paired with construction of a satellite new town to provide housing for displaced central city residents. A new town being added to an existing city may serve the same purpose. While the probable residents of a free-standing new town may not be so easily identified, much is known about the kind of people they will be, based on the proposed population "mix." Participants in the planning of a new town could, therefore, include public trustees for these future residents. As the new town grows, residents could replace the trustees. Such political mechanisms are needed to allow the different yet overlapping interests of residents and nonresidents to be expressed. And in the new town itself some means is needed to phase each wave of new settlers into the political process and to assure that no group becomes entrenched through its early or unequal access to the instruments of power. There is a corresponding need to gradually decrease the control of the developer, whether public or private, over the government; as the population grows residents should assume full responsibility for their own services.

CITIZENSHIP OR CONSUMERSHIP: THE NEW TOWN AS A POLITY

Much of what has been said to this point emphasizes the role of the citizen as a public official of his government. It is a notion contrary to the implicit view of the resident as a consumer, which tends to pervade much thought about both new towns and local government. The new town viewed as a market is a different place from the new town seen as a polity, and the implications of each view for governmental processes are quite different. In the new town as a market, the consumer votes with his money on whether to ratify the developer's and parent government's zoning and building decisions. He has no responsibility, moral or political, for the initial construction. He has no previous stake in the community. He purchases a dwelling unit, and as a consumer he is entitled to receive what he bought—a house plus other amenities. His homeowner's dues are a part of the market transaction, and he is still engaged, as an association member, in a producer-consumer contract. If his home or the amenities prove unsatisfactory, as a consumer he can first complain and seek to demonstrate that it is the producer's responsibility to improve his product. He ultimately retains the right of selling out, probably at a profit, and seeking a better deal elsewhere. As a consumer he is not responsible for the future development of his community, and he has little or no direct and official responsibility for the decisions made about development, population mix and other matters affecting the community at large. His loyalty to the town is essentially customer loyalty, and his principal means of participation are essentially private market mechanisms, however laden they may be with democratic forms and rituals.

This focus on consumership is also congenial to the housekeeping approach to local government. The residents "consume" municipal services. The government is viewed as a producer of services, and it attempts to satisfy consumer demand. As Robert Wood has pointed out, the ideal system for some is a government without politics, a system administered by technicians that serves its customers what they want or are willing to pay for.[23] In such an arrangement feedback in the making of policy can theoretically be handled by an effective complaint bureau. The citizen is a "stockholder" in the enterprise, of course, as well as its customer. The whole arrangement is a little less patronizing than the phone company and a little livelier than the Odd Fellows.

Significant public decisions should not be made by private customers but by public citizens. Citizenship, at least in Western political thought, involves shared responsibility for public acts. Loyalty and participation are derived, ethically and operationally, from this shared responsibility. Contemporary urban and suburban government has tended to erode this concept of citizenship and replace it with consumership. In practice, the citizenry is further and further removed from the actual making of decisions, but because the values of citizenship retain a strong hold on popular imagination the rituals of participation have survived the substance. In practice, "citizens" are encouraged to participate more and more in matters of less and less significance and are condemned as apathetic because they do not. Advisory committees abound and citizen "representatives" are required on all sorts of public boards. New towns seem destined to carry on in the tradition of suburban and city government unless the problem is openly addressed in new-town planning and development.

The new town's government must deal with things that matter. Development of an active and responsible citizenry will depend on the importance of the decisions in which individual citizens can participate. Democracy can be learned only through experience, but the nature of the experience is important. If people perceive that their participation is effective, that it influences or controls public policy and is not an empty gesture, control of the instruments for participation becomes important to those seeking power and advocating programs. Competition for control will develop and attract greater participation. On the other hand, if experience suggests that the forms of participation are shams, that officials neither need nor heed the opinions expressed by citizens through their participatory organs, then the perceived inefficacy of participation will generate apathy, disinterest or counterorganization.

POLITICAL PLURALISM FOR NEW TOWNS

A corollary to the problem of creating a responsible citizenry is that of fostering in new towns a substantive democracy, a democracy based on a pluralistic community containing diverse groups that must tolerate, accommodate and cooperate with each other. New towns will have more diverse populations than conventional suburbs, but they are not likely to be microcosms of the central city or of the metropolitan area in which they are located. Some of Britain's new towns have existed long enough to permit an assessment of their potential for economic and group diversity. Harlow, for instance, attracted a disproportionate number of young families, particularly in its earliest phases of settlement, and a high proportion of scientific and professional people. More than 80 percent of Harlow's work force is employed in the new town itself, a much higher proportion than is projected for America's new towns.

Early experience with new towns in the United States also

suggests that, as in the suburbs, relatively young families that are socially and economically mobile are likely to be early residents. Working class people are more likely to find houses in new towns than in other new suburbs. The proportion of low-income families will depend on the amount of subsidized housing available. So long as the private market supplies the capital for development, most early residents will probably be in the upper-middle-income and upper-income brackets.

The initial residents, by virtue of their education and economic status, are likely to be easily politicized and to include a large number of "cosmopolitans," or civic activists. This was the case in Reston. There, the Reston Citizens Association (RCA) was formed by early residents as a voice for the citizens independent of the developer and as a protector of the new-town plan against modifications by the developer. One of its early and highly successful activities was establishing a commuter bus system for residents working in Washington and in the Pentagon area.[24] The RCA has also been an active political force in dealing with both the developer and the Fairfax County government. Its leaders are "effective citizens" in the tradition of the upper-income suburbs. They are skilled in both bargaining with officials and in doing the technical work so often necessary for negotiating with bureaucracies, public or private.

The close correlation between economic status and participation in community affairs in new towns could diminish as later groups move in or as public bodies begin to promote new towns with larger working class populations. The cosmopolitans are not likely to form lasting alliances with less affluent and less educated neighbors unless such alliances are necessary to control public policy. Since community associations are voluntary, their survival and programs tend to depend on the availability of people with leisure time. Such people are often lacking in working-class or poor neighborhoods unless economic support for indigenous leaders is provided by the spoils system, the antipoverty program, a union or some other means. Political parties may be expected to attract wide participation only in local electoral affairs. Ad hoc group organization and action will most likely be based on what Gans has characterized as "deprivation-oriented" politics—sporadic involvement resulting from threat to status, property or another interest.[25] Local politics will then be ripe for domination by the "professionals," for whom participation offers economic and psychic rewards. If this occurs, new-town politics will be indistinguishable from suburban politics as it has developed since the early 1950s. The prevailing patterns of suburban community participation will tend to be carried over to the new town, but they could be modified by the diversity and character of its population and by planning from the outset political opportunities for furthering a new-town "mission" of creating a working system of democratic pluralism. The goal is not a utopia where everyone participates in everything but a place that actively encourages a wide spectrum of citizens to participate in public affairs and one that can serve as a laboratory for improving the democratic processes of local self-government.

COMMUNITY AND CONFLICT

The new-town mystique is heavily laden with the ideal of "community"—of finding and building on common interests shared by an economically and socially diverse population. This "community" is not likely to be achieved by depending on natural forces and geographic proximity alone. Integrated neighborhoods do not necessarily produce integrated politics or shared interests. A certain sense of community springs naturally from people's realization that they share the experience, frustration, hopes or objectives of their neighbors; but a politically operative community must be maintained by a government capable of inducing diverse groups to act together in mutual self-interest. The potency of local government can be seen in many nondescript towns and incorporated suburbs that lack any physical symbols, even a steeple, but that generate remarkable civic identity, spirit and activity. At a minimum, organization of a new-town government gives citizens an official instrument to use in battles with other units and levels of government or with developers.

A sense of community does not necessarily result in harmonious political relations. To the extent that it succeeds in providing an opportunity for social and economic diversity, the new town has a built-in basis for political conflict. Differing attitudes toward schools, the developer and the development plan, taxes and other matters will generate further conflict. The tendency of new-town groups to identify with the community but to differ on public policy for it increases participation and therefore experience and produces a wider range of policy choices than does a system based on quiet consensus among elites. The problem for many new-town residents will be to rid themselves of the notion that local government should be a fairly sanitary system of consensus on issues. Local government provides only a political framework within which to resolve public issues. Without some kind of governmental system the citizens of new towns may participate somewhat more intensely, but they will lack a framework for resolution of issues and thus can be expected to behave like citizens of other unincorporated suburbs.

THE ABSENCE OF CIVIC HISTORY

The staged development of a new town keeps its political system in constant transition, so its political institutions are likely to appear more unstable than those of older communities. The proportion of new residents will be high for at least half the total development period. The arrangements made for the initial settlers may prove unworkable or unacceptable as the new town grows and reaches a population ten times that of the first stage. Yet once a governmental system is established it will be difficult to adjust it to new circumstances and a more diverse constituency.

The opportunity for creative political experimentation is enhanced by the fact that most new towns have no civic history or traditions, no inherited or established power elite, and consequently lack any well-defined rules for the game of civic conduct. To be sure there is the developer, either private or public, and there is the parent government. But these will gradually be displaced or supplemented, and even in the early stages of development neither is a substitute for local history.

The lack of civic history does not mean that the residents will not carry civic baggage. They will, individually and in groups, have images of politics they will attempt to act out or prevent being acted out,[26] they may have a strong image of what a new town should be, but they will have no common civic model. While most residents will probably have lived nearby, some may come from different states and cities, even from different regions of the country, and surely from different political parties. Some will want to avoid the kind of politics they knew in their previous homes. Others will seek to establish familiar patterns on the new turf. Fitting these diverse political backgrounds to the circumstances of the new towns poses questions never really dealt with in the suburbanization of America, where new residents by and large were poured into old political vessels.

In suburbia the old families often owned the land and the businesses. They could compete fairly well with the new-comers politically, usually maintaining, through their earlier control of institutions, a degree of power in local affairs far greater than their numbers might warrant. The new town will have few, if any, established family and business leaders. Business, at least substantial business, will quite likely be absentee owned and managed. The first wave of new-towners will be old-timers within two years, when the second or third group of houses will open for occupancy. The pace of development in most new towns is apt to be such that the population will increase annually by 100 percent during each of the first two or three years and by 50 percent annually for the next several years. Not until the town is well over half built can its population be expected to change by as little as 10 to 20 percent a year. Physical and social assimilation of these repeated waves of new residents is complicated enough; to adjust the political system to the consequent electoral and group instability is even more complex. In any of the first three quadrennia, a majority of the electorate will be voting in its first election. While this circumstance produces an atmosphere of political instability, it does not necessarily mean that institutions will change or adjust accordingly.

The new town, since it is planned as a whole, offers an opportunity to experiment with the persistent problem of how to let political institutions grow and change incrementally with the population. The problem involves not only governmental institutions and processes but private institutions as well. Churches, charitable and voluntary organizations, semi-official neighborhood groups and political parties all affect the way in which the political system functions. Their combined influence may render the early assumptions made (or not made) about political life in the town outdated or inadequate by the time it is half built or completed. Thus one of the central issues of governing a new town is whether it can offer experience in developing new institutions that not only can overcome the most glaring deficiencies of existing local governments but can cope with the political consequences of the process of urbanization. The new town gives its residents a chance to reduce the lag between social and technological change and the adjustment of institutions to those changes.

What Kind of Government?

It is against this backdrop that government for new towns must be understood. New towns can try new approaches to the problems of community political development that now plague both the central cities and the suburbs. Initially lacking the inertia that characterizes city governments and with more varied populations than the conventional suburbs, new towns offer an opportunity almost unparalleled in American urban development to experiment with new approaches to effective citizen participation, new ways of sharing experience and responsibility for governing and new ways of managing the conflicting interests that make claims on public resources.

Providing new towns some standard forms of government to choose from will not meet this challenge. New governmental forms will be required to meet the needs of development and to further the physical and social goals of the many new towns to house several million people that will be built as a consequence of the passage of the 1970 housing act and the quickened interest in new-town development at all levels of government. Much can be learned from the experience of existing new towns in attempting to adapt old governmental forms to their needs, but those seeking new forms of democratic expression for the citizens of new towns cannot be bound by this experience as an inevitable pattern for the future.

As new towns become integral parts of state and national urban growth policies, they will have to reflect publicly determined standards. Variety in housing and racial integration are already important considerations in federal assistance to new-town developers. As instruments of public policy in relocating industry and population from overcrowded cities, new towns will become subject to even more influence by public agencies. It seems likely that, spurred by federal assistance, state public bodies will become major developers of new towns, as may federal agencies themselves, some years hence. With increased public participation, the necessity for democratic accountability will also increase. But, notwithstanding the obvious public interest involved, governments have not formulated policies and procedures specifically relating to the governmental problems of new towns. State laws, which regulate the creation of political subdivisions and the powers to be extended to them, have not been modified to reflect new-town needs.

New towns require not only internal political mechanisms for democratic self-government and providing public services, but mechanisms for relating to the parent jurisdictions in which they are located and for resolving conflicts with those jurisdictions. They must also have the means of integrating new settlers into the political process and of assuring that no group can achieve an entrenched position through its early or unequal access to governmental institutions.

Experience of existing new towns suggests basic guidelines for achieving these goals.

First, development of governmental institutions ought not be left to private industry alone, or to happenstance. There is a legitimate public interest in defining standards for physical development to assure that new towns are prepared to cope with significant urban problems and to foster better approaches to local self-government. State governments will need to revise their laws regarding local governments and special districts to permit governmental development of new towns to keep pace with their physical growth. They will also need to consider whether the heavy public investment in new towns justifies making mandatory some of the means of public participation in the planning and development process discussed in this paper—that is, writing into law at least minimum requirements for citizen participation in each phase of new-town development. Special attention should also be given the status, stability and implications for local democracy of private governments in new towns. Because of their special responsibilities for services and as community catalysts they are often useful interim governments or parallel institutions to public agencies, so their structure, membership and control require close attention.

Second, the primary focus of this paper has been on how the processes of governing new towns and of developing responsible citizens are affected by both the physical and institutional environment. For new towns to fulfill their democratic promise, public agencies and private developers will need to understand and accept the notion that the new town should enhance democratic values and broaden opportunity for meaningful participation in public life. This suggests not only a need for providing initial structures and open doors, but affirmative programs of community education, taxation and organization that will assure to citizens political power and authority over programs.

Experimentation is needed to establish workable patterns that will give the new towns of America's future a real chance to fulfill Mumford's vision:

> Political life, instead of being the monopoly of remote specialists, must become as constant a process in daily living as the housewife's visit to the grocer or the butcher, and more frequent than the man's visit to the barber. If the leisure that man has been promised by the machine counts for anything, it must count for the extension of the privilege of being an active political animal.[27]

Notes

1. "New community," the term used in the act, is often used interchangeably with the term "new town," which is used throughout this report for uniformity and clarity.

2. The author of this paper gratefully acknowledges the assistance of Kathryn Stone, Senior Associate of the Washington Center for Metropolitan Studies, who aided in the research and in the development of the underlying ideas. The members of the task force offered suggestions and criticisms of earlier drafts, as did Henry Bain and Eric Freund.

3. See Mary J. Mullarkey, "The Evolution of a New Community: Problems of Government," *Harvard Journal on Legislation*, 1968–69, pp. 463–68.

4. Fred L. Wenner, *The Story of Oklahoma and the 89'ers*, Co-operative Publishing Company, Guthrie, Oklahoma, 1939.

5. Ebenezer Howard, *Garden Cities of Tomorrow*, S. Sonnenschein and Co. Ltd., London, 1902 (first issued in 1898 under the title *Tomorrow: A Peaceful Path to Real Reform*, reprinted under its present title by MIT Press, Cambridge, Mass., 1965).

6. See Lewis Mumford, *The Culture of Cities*, Harcourt, Brace & World, New York, 1938, especially pp. 392–401; Clarence Stein, *Toward New Towns for America*, Liverpool University Press, Liverpool, 1951 (reprinted by MIT Press, Cambridge, Mass., 1966).

7. The most prominent of these plans was National Capital Planning Commission and National Capital Regional Planning Council, *A Policies Plan for the Year 2000: The Nation's Capital*, Washington, 1961. The Baltimore Regional Planning Council's *Metrotowns for the Baltimore Region: A Pattern Emerges*, Baltimore, 1962, also argued for the creation of satellite cities.

8. Donald Canty, ed., *The New City*, Praeger, New York, 1969, pp. 172 ff.

9. For instance, William Alfonso, "The Mirage of New Towns," *The Public Interest*, Spring 1970, pp. 3–17.

10. Harvey S. Perloff, "New Towns In-Town," *Journal of the American Institute of Planners,* May 1966, pp. 155–61.

11. Metropolitan Fund, Inc., *Regional New Town Design: A Paired Community for Southeast Michigan,* Detroit, 1971.

12. Paul Ylvisaker, "Socio-Political Innovations and New Communities," paper presented at Conference on Innovation and New Communities, Princeton University, September 28, 1970.

13. Public service grants, provided by Title VII of the 1970 housing act, alleviate this problem for some new towns. Zoning and licensing ordinances may also provide a means of requiring the developer to meet certain standards of service.

14. This pattern will change somewhat as developers take advantage of provisions of the 1970 housing act authorizing the federal government to guarantee loans for land assembly and development and to make loans to pay interest on "front-end" money. With few exceptions, however, land assembly will remain a private market process.

15. Stein, *op. cit.,* pp. 61–64.

16. Louis Brownlow, *A Passion for Politics,* University of Chicago Press, Chicago, 1958, pp. 218–20.

17. The covenants were developed on the basis of a year of research by Charles Ascher. Charles Ascher, "The Extra-Municipal Administration of Radburn: An Experiment in Government by Contract," *National Municipal Review,* no. 442, July 1929; *idem.,* "Private Covenants," in *Urban Redevelopment: Problems and Practices,* ed. Coleman Woodbury, University of Chicago Press, Chicago, 1953, pp. 226–308.

18. Stanley Scott, "The Homes Association: Will 'Private Government' Serve the Public Interest?" *Public Affairs Report,* Bulletin of the Institute of Governmental Studies, University of California, Berkeley, February 1967.

19. Albert A. Foer, "Democracy in the New Towns: The Limits of Private Government," *University of Chicago Law Review,* 1969, pp. 397–412.

20. Stanley Scott, "The Large New Communities: Ultimate Self-Government and Other Problems," *Public Affairs Report,* Bulletin of the Institute of Governmental Studies, University of California, Berkeley, October 1965; *idem.,* "Urban Growth Challenges New Towns," *Public Management,* September 1966, pp. 253–60.

21. Herbert Gans describes the governmental process in Levittown in *The Levittowners,* Pantheon Books, New York, 1967, pp. 333–403. See also Gans, "Planning and Political Participation," *Journal of the American Institute of Planners,* 1953, p. 6.

22. Howard W. Hallman, *Neighborhood Control of Public Programs,* Praeger, New York, 1970, pp. 206–18.

23. Robert Wood, *Suburbia: Its People, Their Politics,* Houghton Mifflin, Boston, 1959, pp. 194–97.

24. Henry Bain, *The Reston Bus,* Washington Center for Metropolitan Studies, Washington, 1969.

25. Gans, *op. cit.,* pp. 7–8.

26. *Ibid.*

27. Mumford, *op. cit.,* pp. 382–83.